COACHING COMPANIES

To Greater
Sales & Profits

COACHING COMPANIES
To Greater Sales & Profits

366 Sales Leadership Action Items

JACK DALY

PSCI Publishing
La Jolla, California

Coaching Companies To Greater Sales & Profits
366 Sales Leadership Action Items

Jack Daly

Published by:
PSCI Publishing
5842 La Jolla Corona Drive
La Jolla, CA 92037

Phone: (888) 298-6868
Fax: (858) 454-5481
www.ProfessionalSalesCoach.net

Cover design and inside layout: Ad Graphics, Inc., Tulsa, OK
Printed in the United States of America

ISBN: 0-9712126-1-9

WHAT OTHERS ARE SAYING ABOUT JACK DALY...

"Your insights and observations were right on target with our group. In fact, the sound strategies and thoughtful techniques that you shared with us can only be surpassed by the contagious energy and enthusiasm that charged your presentation from beginning to end."

Sharon L. Allen, Managing Partner
Deloitte & Touche

"What rave reviews you received for your presentation earlier this month at the RPMA conference. The comments I got were that everyone wanted more, one hour simply wasn't enough time. This is the 12th year for the conference, and I think yours was the best review I've received in all 12 years."

Vicki Miller, Executive Director
RPMA

"I didn't need to tell you what it takes to hold the attention of an 'all CEO' group such as mine, because you did it. All too often speakers come from theory without practice. Your background indicated 'you've been there' and your presentation showed for it. The most frequent comment heard was the amount of immediately implementable action ideas delivered."

Dick Swanson, Chairman
The Executives Committee, (TEC)

"Wow! I can't get your program out of my head. All the management training I have had over the years condensed, bottled, shook up and sprayed all over the room in a one hour shower! Like good champagne."

David Peters
Principal, Architectural Security Group

"What an inspiring presentation! Your speech was the perfect tonic. People throughout the company have been talking about it for weeks. They recognize amongst themselves a renewed commitment and excitement. Your stories and examples gave evidence of a real grasp for our business—it was clear you did your homework . . . with so much to offer, we want you back."

Gordon Stockwell
President, ICI

THIS BOOK IS DEDICATED TO:

Entrepreneurs everywhere . . . may their businesses grow better, their associates work smarter, and everyone involved in the business of business have fun on the journey towards greater sales and profits!

"A short saying often contains much wisdom."
– Sophocles (c. 450 B.C.)

ACKNOWLEDGMENTS

I've had the good fortune to have worked with more than my fair share of successful business leaders. As so often happens, many evolved to be close friends. Here are a few who had significant impact on me and my thinking. My partners at Platinum Capital Group, Mark Moses and Brett Dillenberg, whose behavior exemplifies entrepreneurialism; Jim Pratt, who opened my eyes to the professional world of sales and the art of sharing such knowledge; Gerry Layo, hands down one of the best sales professionals I've worked with; Ed Kahn, for lessons in grace under pressure and personal integrity; Jon Tilley, by demonstrating the power of a compelling vision and raising the bar of personal potential; Stan Sanderson, who taught me the lessons of a professional business coach, and the importance of measurement and accountability; and Mitch Safran, for teaching me at an early age that all employees and customers are not equal and that some deserve more attention and recognition than others. There have been many others who have positively influenced me as well, and I thank them all.

Additionally, there are two particular CEO groups I've had the pleasure of working with for a number of years that have added tremendous value to me both professionally and personally. The Young

Entrepreneurs Organization (YEO) and The Executive Committee (TEC) have fostered many friendships, given birth to many business building ideas and saved me from unnecessary expenses. The members have demonstrated the valued "3 C's" of organizations of their purpose—commitment, confidentiality, and caring. Many of the lessons shared in this book have resulted from my associations with these folks.

Last but not least, thanks to the people "behind the scenes." They include Eric Figi at Professional Sales Coach, Inc. and Platinum Capital Group's various Directors of First Impressions, who so often are the "face" of our companies to our clients. Thanks for your professionalism and support.

PS. A special thanks to Jim and Barbara Weems of AD Graphics who helped with my first book, *Daily Sales Motivators*, which led to me working with them earlier than expected on this project.

INTRODUCTION

I don't pretend to have all the answers. In fact, it seems the more I learn, the more I discover just how much I don't know. For over twenty years now, I've been assembling and creating business axioms which serve to reinforce my day to day leadership activities. Here, then, are daily reminders (kicks in the seat of the pants). I hope they serve to stimulate you and your business.

Jack Daly

COACHING COMPANIES

To Greater Sales & Profits

366 Sales Leadership Action Items

#1 January 1

Once you have decided on your mission, go for it as if your life depended on it. Sell your vision with evangelistic fervor. Your conviction will be contagious.

#2 January 2

Jack Welch's six rules:
1) Face reality as it is, not as it was or as you wish it to be.
2) Be candid with everyone.
3) Don't manage, lead.
4) Change before you have to.
5) If you don't have a competitive advantage, don't compete.
6) Control your own destiny, or someone else will.

#3 January 3

A sales manager's job is not to grow sales. A sales manager's job is to grow sales people—in quantity and quality.

Jack Daly

#4 January 4

What separates the entrepreneurs from others is that entrepreneurs act on what they see.

William B. Gartner

#5 January 5

10 Commandments of Speed

1. Focus on the customer—he signs everybody's paycheck.

2. Get in step with the future—that's where opportunity lies.

3. Be an innovator—in an era of rapid change, continuous improvement through innovation is king.

4. Do it with quality—it lowers costs, increases speed, builds pride, and improves customer loyalty.

5. Get rapid, accurate feedback—know what your customers, competitors, employees, suppliers, and the market are doing. Ignorance can be fatal.

6. Ability means agility—be flexible and quick to respond and adapt.

7. If it doesn't add value, don't do it—any job or activity that doesn't build value is creating needless overhead. Don't do it; get rid of it.

8. Build teams, not empires—cross-functional work teams make better, faster decisions than bureaucracies.

9. Lifelong learning is everybody's job—if you want to stay gainfully employed in a rapidly changing world, learn how to learn and keep learning.

10. Just Do It!—Now!—set challenging deadlines that force yourself and others to use time in the most efficient and effective manner.

Michael Leboeuf

#6 January 6

The best training in the world won't change your sales force if it is contradicted by supervision or by the reward system.

Neil Rackham

#7 January 7

Most people come to work well prepared, well motivated and wanting to reach their potential. A primary issue today is helping managers understand that it's not their job to supervise or to motivate but to liberate and enable. You have to look at leadership through the eyes of followers. Lech Walesa told Congress that there is a declining world market for words. He's right. The only thing the world believes is behavior, because we all see it instantaneously. None of us may preach anymore. We must behave.

Max DePree

#8 January 8

To maximize the impact of extrinsic rewards, make them personal, immediate, and public: PIP.

Robert Kriegel

#9 January 9

Every day at IBM was a day devoted to business development, not doing business. We didn't do business at IBM, we built one.

Tom Watson

#10 January 10

How many of your associates are overly recognized? Implement consistent recognition systems.

#11 January 11

To use a mission statement effectively, you must: Enroll, Empower, Recognize.

#12 January 12

It may be a cliché but it's true: you play at the level of your practice, the best way is to practice hard all the time.

Don Shula

#13 January 13

Did you teach, counsel, or motivate someone today? Did you provide a blast of energy, electricity, and excitement today?

#14 January 14

People judge your company on everything imaginable, especially the way you handle phone messages. If you knew a multimillion dollar order rode on the way you answered the phone, would you change anything?

David Armstrong

#15 January 15

Act quickly but don't hurry.

John Wooden

#16 January 16

It is the responsibility of a leader to get along with each of his/her associates—not their responsibility to get along with the leader.

#17 January 17

A leader is best when people barely know he exists.

Not so good when people obey and acclaim him.

Worse when they despise him.

If you fail to honor people, they fail to honor you.

But of a good leader, who talks little, when his work is done, his aim fulfilled, they will say "we did this ourselves!"

Lao-Tse

#18 January 18

A successful sales culture understands the value of having that culture driven by "relationships developed" instead of "transactions completed."

#19 January 19

Recruiting is a pro-active process, not a responsive solution.

#20 January 20

Speed is useful only if you are running in the right direction.

Joel A. Barker

#21 January 21

Business development is everybody's responsibility.

Gary Wendt

#22 January 22

Everyone in the first thirty days wonders if they have made a mistake in joining your group. Communicate regularly to overcome this.

#23 January 23

I don't meet competition, I crush it.

Charles Revson

#24 January 24

There is more potential in working with your high performers than your low performers. Make the pacesetters in your company the winners, not the losers.

Stephen J. Mulvany

#25 January 25

Without a leader committed to learning, an organization will never approach its potential for success.

#26 January 26

You can achieve more with a "we will" attitude as a leader-manager than a "you will" attitude.

#27 January 27

Think, believe, dream, dare. Don't aim too low.

Walt Disney

#28 January 28

Marketing is too important to be left to the marketing department.

David Packard

#29 January 29

Visionary companies focus primarily on beating themselves . . . relentlessly asking the question, "How can we improve ourselves to do better tomorrow than we did today?"

James C. Collins /Jerry I. Porras

#30 January 30

In baseball and business, the needs of the team are best met when we meet the needs of individual persons.

Max Depree

#31 January 31

Be an enthusiastic leader—you are the message.

#32 February 1

Minimum standards of performance should be negotiated with each individual associate.

Jack Daly

#33 February 2

Identify role models and mentors. Align the new with the experienced.

#34 February 3

The most expensive time in a manager's life is the time between when you truly lose faith in someone and when you do something about it.

#35 February 4

Customer contact is the lifeblood of sales.

Frank Pacetta

#36 February 5

Orchestrate at least monthly sales meetings, addressing improvement of sales skills.

#37 February 6

Have each sales person establish and carry a "target list" of where—specifically—his/her business will come from in the next twelve months.

#38 February 7

Slaying sacred cows makes great steaks.

Dick Nicolosi

#39 February 8

There's as much risk in doing nothing as in doing something.

Trammell Crow

#40 February 9

Question No. 1 for the prospective business owner (should be): In 25 words or less, how is my concept notably different from that of others? If you can't succinctly explain how you're special to "the man or woman on the street," you're headed for trouble.

Tom Peters

#41 February 10

Remember, I don't care how much you know until I know how much you care.

#42 February 11

Employ the "Gretzky Factor" —Be moving to where the puck is going and not to where it is.

#43 February 12

People will live up to your expectations or down to your level of distrust.

Jim Pratt

#44 February 13

In whatever you do . . . make sure there is a "wow factor," something that will grab people's attention and make them notice that you've sweated the details.

Carl Sewell

#45 February 14

When someone says that they are going to resign in order to join you, coach your recruit to answer this question: "What are you going to say in response to their efforts to keep you?"

Jack Daly

#46 February 15

Every organization has to prepare for the abandonment of everything it does.

Peter Drucker

#47 February 16

The best way to avoid problems is not to hire them.

#48 February 17

Implementation is bottom-up, commitment and support are top-down.

#49 February 18

Change is inevitable, growth is optional.

#50 February 19

Avoid making decisions your employees can make.

#51 February 20

Winners love to be measured. Only losers hate numbers. They don't want to be held accountable for their actions.

Richard C. Rose

#52 February 21

The day (people) stop bringing you their problems is the day you have stopped leading them. They have either lost confidence that you can help them or concluded that you do not care. Either case is a failure of leadership. If this were a litmus test, the majority of CEO's would fail. One, they build so many barriers to upward communication that the very idea of someone lower in the hierarchy looking up to the leader for help is ludicrous. Two, the corporate culture they foster often defines asking for help as weakness or failure, so people cover up their gaps, and the organization suffers accordingly. Real leaders make themselves accessible and available. They show concern for the efforts and challenges faced by underlings—even as they demand high standards. Accordingly, they are more likely to create an environment where problem analysis replaces blame.

Colin Powell

#53 February 22

A good sales strategy is to grow your business with the customers you already have.

#54 February 23

Recruiting is a lot like shaving. You miss a day and you look like a bum.

Jackie Sherrill

#55 February 24

Some executives create more enthusiasm when they leave a room than when they enter it. Which are you?

#56 February 25

Shun the incremental and go for the leap.

Jack Welch

#57 February 26

Call your office at least once a month and ask yourself "What is the quality of our first impression?"

#58 February 27

You must manage as if you need your employees more than they need you.

Peter Drucker

#59 February 28

Winning companies focus on rewarding stars, cutting dead wood.

Andrall E. Pearson

#60 February 29

If no one is ever at work at 6:00 AM or 8:00 PM, your company is in trouble.

#61 March 1

Make a list of your 100 top customers. Put it in your desk drawer. Every week call four of them, just to check in, listen, see if there's anything they want to talk about. Anything. When you get to the bottom of the list, start all over again from the top.

Tom Peters

#62 March 2

It's not the people you fire who make your life miserable; it's the people you don't fire who make your life miserable.

#63 March 3

Share success with the people who make it happen. It makes everybody think like an owner, which helps them build long-term relationships with customers and influences them to do things in an efficient way.

Emily Ericsen

#64 March 4

Recruiting is a process, not an event. It must be ongoing and continuous.

Jack Daly

#65 March 5

Praise loudly and criticize quietly.

#66 March 6

Pay for results. Pay for performance, but don't pay for effort.

Ralph Parilla

#67 March 7

In the race for success, the speed of the leader determines the pace of the pack.

#68 March 8

More people should learn to tell their dollars where to go instead of asking where they went.

Roger W. Babson

#69 March 9

If you don't treat your own people well, they won't treat other people well.

Herb Kelleher

#70 March 10

Customization is the future. Give each customer what they want, the way they want it.

#71 March 11

The best ideas for improving a job come from those who do it every day.

#72 March 12

The basic responsibility of the CEO is to design the game and arrange the talent.

Renn Zaphiropoulos

#73 March 13

If you want one year of prosperity, grow grain. If you want ten years of prosperity, grow trees. If you want one hundred years of prosperity, grow people.

Old Chinese Proverb

#74 March 14

As a manager the important thing is not what happens when you are there, but what happens when you are not there.

Ken Blanchard

#75 March 15

If you see a snake, just kill it. Don't appoint a committee on snakes.

H. Ross Perot

#76 March 16

They watch your feet, not your lips.

Tom Peters

#77 March 17

Caring is contagious; spread it around.

Jack Daly

#78 March 18

Authentic feedback flows in all directions.

#79 March 19

You are not really managing unless you have a plan to periodically "inspect" results yourself.

Guy Arvia

#80 March 20

Knowledgeable companies communicate.

#81 March 21

Let people accomplish your objectives their way.

Clark Johnson

#82 March 22

When you change the perception from closing a sale to opening a new client, you have taught the salesperson to thrive for a lifetime.

Gerry Layo

#83 March 23

No statue was ever erected to the memory of a person who thought it best to leave well enough alone.

#84 March 24

"Ain't none of us as smart as all of us." Get the whole team involved.

#85 March 25

Name one person you've ever fired "too soon."

Ken Kelly

#86 March 26

Early established habits are difficult to change— make them positive ones.

#87 March 27

The secret to successfully managing people is to understand what they really want out of their careers and then give it to them.

#88 March 28

Be as nice as you can be, and as un-nice as you have to be.

Harvey Mackay

#89 March 29

The window to the future gives better guidance than the mirror. Focus on actions with your associates going forward.

#90 March 30

Go after the 80 percent on each initiative and forget the remaining 20 percent—it's rarely worth the extra effort.

#91 March 31

When considering a candidate as a new hire, ask yourself:

Would I look forward to sitting side-by-side with him or her on a coast-to-coast flight?

Would I want to have dinner with this person outside of the interview forum?

#92 April 1

An empowered associate does not need to be motivated, managed, or leveraged with top-down power.

Kraig Kramers

#93 April 2

So much of what we call management consists of making it difficult for people to work.

Peter Drucker

#94 April 3

When people you respect recommend books, read them.

#95 April 4

Don't hire only people who look and act like you. A mix will create a more effective team.

#96 April 5

Organization change will not occur unless your associates believe it is in their best interest to do so.

#97 April 6

Your sales people should be optimistic, energetic cheerleaders. If they're not, changes are necessary (and not necessarily with them).

#98 April 7

Executive ability is the talent for deciding something quickly and getting somebody else to do it.

Red Scott

#99 April 8

People are different, lead accordingly.

#100 April 9

People love applause—offer it generously.

#101 April 10

If more CEO'S had to go out and sell their products, day in and out, they'd pay a lot more attention to what they were making. When you're out there selling, there's no place to hide. It's the acid test.

Jim Koch

#102 April 11

You cannot motivate other people, but you can put them in an environment where they will motivate themselves.

#103 April 12

If your goal is satisfied clients, your goal is far too modest.

#104 April 13

Life and business are like the carpool lane. The best way to reach your destination quickly is to take some people with you.

Pete Ward

#105 April 14

You can buy a person's time and talent—but loyalty and enthusiasm you must earn.

#106 April 15

Search for eagles and then teach them to fly in formation.

D. Wayne Calloway

#107 April 16

If you're too busy to help those around you succeed, you're too busy!

Bob Moawad

#108 April 17

Trust each other again and again. When the trust level gets high enough, people transcend apparent limits, discovering new and awesome abilities for which they were previously unaware.

David Armistead

#109 April 18

If you bungle raising your children, I don't think whatever else you do well matters very much.

Jacqueline Kennedy Onassis

#110 April 19

Business is a game of intensity and emotion. Deliver both.

#111 April 20

The job of the enterprise is to provide an exciting atmosphere that's open and fair, where people have the resources to go out and win. The job of the people is to take advantage of this playing field and put out 110 percent.

Jack Welch

#112 April 21

Business must be run at a profit, else it will die. But when anyone tries to run a business solely for profit . . . then also the business must die, for it no longer has a reason for existence.

Henry Ford

#113 April 22

Start every sales meeting with a standing ovation. Prioritize recognition.

#114 April 23

The first responsibility of a leader is to define a vision. The last is to say "thank you." In between the leader is a servant.

Max DePree

#115 April 24

Empowerment :

Is it right for the customer?

Is it right for the company?

Is it ethical?

Is it something for which you are willing to be accountable?

Is it consistent with our company's basic beliefs?

If the answer is "yes" to all five questions, don't ask, JUST DO IT!

Rick Rose

#116 April 25

Your associates came to work with your company for their reasons. Find out what they are and work to help them be successful.

#117 April 26

A salesman, like the battery in your car, is constantly discharging energy. Unless he is recharged at frequent intervals he soon runs dry. This is one of the greatest responsibilities of sales leadership.

Richard Grant

#118 April 27

Every leader should do progress reviews (not formal annual performance reviews) with his or her associates at least every quarter.

#119 April 28

Every leader should have a recruiting target list, identified from one's networking efforts.

#120 April 29

If your business keeps you so busy that you have no time for anything else, there must be something wrong, either with you or with your business.

William J. H. Boetcker

#121 April 30

If you don't have a goal for your company—a goal that you can describe in a phrase or a sentence—you really don't know where you're going.

Charles Garfield

#122 May 1

Recruiting is the never-ending process of looking for qualified candidates for employment.

#123 May 2

My experience has shown me that the people who are exceptionally good in business aren't so because of what they know but because of their insatiable need to know more.

Michael E. Gerber

#124 May 3

Hire smart—as opposed to managing hard.

#125 May 4

Do three things each year that will make a difference in your business. Know what they are and stick with them.

Tom Laco

#126 May 5

The moment a manager decides that he/she can change someone—after hiring—the manager has become a social worker and not a manager.

Jim Pratt

#127 May 6

As soon as the decision to hire has been made and the employment offer accepted, ORDER BUSINESS CARDS.

#128 May 7

Recognition is so easy to do and so inexpensive to distribute that there is simply no excuse for not doing it.

Rosabeth Moss Kanter

#129 May 8

Never start someone until you have the personal time to commit to an effective orientation/welcome.

#130 May 9

Market share is an anachronism. What drives success today is market responsiveness.

John Thorbeck

#131 May 10

The typical sales force finds that only 20 to 30 percent of their time is spent on revenue-producing areas, while the most tightly managed sales force gets closer to 40 or 50 percent. Consider it this way. . . you can have the same selling capacity with half the number of people and expense.

Neil Rackham

#132 May 11

Implement a first day celebration for all new hires. Make it an event!

#133 May 12

If you want to know what people want, ask them— and listen to what they say.

David Armstrong

#134 May 13

Positive reinforcement of those things people do right will do more to create a success environment than "constructive criticism."

#135 May 14

Your group goals will be higher if you start from the bottom up rather than imposing quotas from the top down.

#136 May 15

Growing your way to success is a lot more fun than cutting your way to success.

Tom Dunham

#137 May 16

Compensation reviews are for past performance; progress reviews are for future commitment.

#138 May 17

There are an enormous number of managers who have retired on the job.

Peter Drucker

#139 May 18

If you add a report, take one away.

#140 May 19

Send a personal corporate update communication via voicemail or audio-cassette to each sales person at least monthly.

#141 May 20

Establish continuous recognition systems. Never go home without praising someone in the sales force and company for what they did.

#142 May 21

You don't have to be perfect, just better than the competition.

#143 May 22

Unfortunately, the most common thing to happen to the good performer is nothing at all.

Stephen J. Mulvany

#144 May 23

If you resist change, you can only fall further behind.

If you merely go along with change, you will only keep pace with it.

If you create change, you will be the one to dominate and lead it.

#145 May 24

Authority is 20% given and 80% taken. A leader has to assume complete and total responsibility.

Peter Uberroth

#146 May 25

Are you a technician or a cheerleader? How do you spend your time?

#147 May 26

If you didn't fire 'em, rehire 'em.

Bill Fromm

#148 May 27

For increased sales production, spend more time at the top, and less at the bottom.

#149 May 28

Don't tell employees how to do the job . . . tell them what needs to be done.

#150 May 29

A boss that is interested in what employees have to say will not state his/her own opinions first.

#151 May 30

Never delegate responsibility without authority.

#152 May 31

The best job for an employee who constantly says, "Because that's the way we've always done it," is with one of your competitors.

#153 June 1

When interviewing a new candidate, ask yourself how you'd feel if this person were working for your largest competitor rather than you.

#154 June 2

Get the operation up and running while the competition is still in bed.

Frank Pacetta

#155 June 3

Of all the things I've done, the most vital is coordinating the talents of those who work for us and pointing them toward a certain goal.

Walter E. Disney

#156 June 4

What the leader says is important, what the leader does is critical.

#157 June 5

Trying to downsize a business into prosperity is an exercise in futility.

#158 June 6

Leadership is the ability to have a vision and to see that vision through to its end.

Jim Garrison

#159 June 7

People are down on what they are not up on— Communicate!

#160 June 8

Be like the company that keeps one chair empty at all management meetings. The chair is for the customer who should have a say in all policy decisions.

John Schuster

#161 June 9

People don't work for companies; they work at companies. People work for themselves and their friends—their "family." Create a family environment and productivity will noticeably improve.

Jack Daly

#162 June 10

If your company is doing well, double your training budget; if your company is not doing well, quadruple it.

Tom Peters

#163 June 11

In a time of drastic change, it is the learners who inherit the future. The learned find themselves equipped to live in a world that no longer exists.

Eric Hoffer

#164 June 12

No one ever achieved greatness by playing it safe.

Harry Gray

#165 June 13

Commit people to getting the results, but then let them determine the best methods and means.

#166 June 14

You can dream, create, design, and build the most wonderful idea in the world, but it requires people to make the dream a reality.

Walt Disney

#167 June 15

Each day, at some point, stop and ask yourself, "Is what I'm doing moving me toward my goals? Is it a priority?"

#168 June 16

There is no limit to what a person can do or where that person can go if he or she doesn't mind who gets the credit.

#169 June 17

What is impossible to do, but if it could be done, would fundamentally change your business? Ask the question often, of everyone, listen to the answers.

Joel A. Barker

#170 June 18

Periodically ask your sales people, "What is the one thing that the company or I can do to help you advance professionally?" Don't assume you know the answer.

Joe Petrone

#171 June 19

Just as athletes are attracted to winning teams, so it is with employees in business.

#172 June 20

If work goals and the criteria for success are not clear, everyone will guess. Be specific.

#173 June 21

The most valuable of all capital is that invested in human beings.

Alfred Marshall

#174 June 22

If you want to be a big company tomorrow, you have to start acting like one today.

Thomas J. Watson, Jr.

#175 June 23

You generally need to change only one thing to turn an average performer into a top performer—their attitude. Caution—it can be the toughest job of all.

#176 June 24

I never give any credence to anybody whose butt is the same shape as their desk chair.

Dirty Harry

#177 June 25

To promote cooperation and teamwork remember: People tend to resist what is forced upon them. People tend to support that which they helped to create.

Vince Pfaff

#178 June 26

The best minute you spend is the one you invest in your people.

Blanchard & Johnson

#179 June 27

Success. To laugh often and much; to win the respect of intelligent people and the affection of children; to earn the appreciation of honest critics and endure the betrayal of false friends; to appreciate beauty, to find the best in others; to leave the world a bit better, whether by a healthy child, a garden patch or a redeemed social condition; to know even one life has breathed easier because you have lived. This is to have succeeded.

Ralph Waldo Emerson

#180 June 28

Culture is one of the most precious things a company has, so you must work harder at it than anything else.

Herb Kelleher

#181 June 29

There is something that is much more scarce, something rarer than ability. It is the ability to recognize ability.

Robert Half

#182 June 30

It's easier for people to see it your way if you first
see it their way.

Jack Kaine

#183 July 1

Be careful—a little success can create a lot of
overhead.

Red Scott

#184 July 2

See everything; overlook a great deal; correct a little.

Pope John XXIII

#185 July 3

The world of the 1990's and beyond will not belong
to "managers" who can make the numbers dance.
The world will belong to passionate, driven leaders—
people who not only have enormous amounts of
energy but who can energize those whom they lead.

Jack Welch

#186 July 4

Staffing is the most important decision you or your
managers will ever make. When you have good
people, your company can do anything.

Ed Ryan

#187 July 5

Seek alignment: When individuals perceive that contributing to the group is a WIN/WIN relationship contributing to their personal missions.

#188 July 6

Employees who aren't given information can't assume responsibility. Employers who are given information can't avoid assuming it.

Jack Stack

#189 July 7

Institute "cascading mission statements"—where each department/location/associate participates in the mission creation.

#190 July 8

For each job position, define the profile of the ideal candidate.

#191 July 9

People don't mind being supported or led, but many do mind being "managed." If you must manage something, manage the process.

John McNeil

#192 July 10

If you hire mediocre sales persons, the top producers lose their challenge. If you hire top producers, you create healthy competition.

#193 July 11

When you go to work tomorrow, try to look at "your place" as a fearful, first day employee would. Would you want your son or daughter to work there?

Tom Peters

#194 July 12

Companies must burn themselves down and rebuild every few years.

Roger Martin

#195 July 13

Hell, there ain't no rules. We are trying to accomplish something.

Thomas Edison

#196 July 14

How can I best deploy my resources—human, physical, and financial? What are the best opportunities both for the short and long terms?

Thomas Horton

#197 July 15

Most people fail not because of technical knowledge but because of attitude or people skills problems.

#198 July 16

Successful hiring requires, "If in doubt—SAY NO."

#199 July 17

The only thing of real importance that leaders do is to create and manage culture and that the unique talent of leaders is their ability to work with culture.

Edgar H. Schein

#200 July 18

If you recruit people who are smarter than you are, you prove that you are smarter than they are.

#201 July 19

Never leave well enough alone. Others certainly won't, and that affects everybody. That is why it is more important to ask "what's new?" than "how's business?"—"how's business?" is about the past, but "what's new?" is about the future.

Theodore Levitt

#202 July 20

The office image and work commitment created in the first month, first day, and first hour is difficult to change. Make it a positive one.

#203 July 21

Elephants have a hard time adapting. Cockroaches outlive everything.

Peter Drucker

#204 July 22

Help each new hire to be successful early after they join you. Assign a peer as a buddy for 60 days.

#205 July 23

The message is clear: (1) Trust, (2) "They" can handle "it" (whatever "it" is), (3) You're only in control when you're out of control.

Tom Peters

#206 July 24

Everyone is entitled to know where he/she stands and how they are progressing. To avoid a problem is to court disaster.

#207 July 25

Work as hard preparing for the progress review to determine positives to reinforce as you do to define negatives to correct.

#208 July 26

The main thing is to keep the main thing the main thing.

Steven Covey

#209 July 27

The mediocre teacher tells. The good teacher explains. The superior teacher demonstrates. The great teacher inspires.

#210 July 28

Regularly conducted progress reviews either will "fire up" your associates, or "fire out" those not performing to the level of expectation.

#211 July 29

A smart businessperson is one who makes a mistake, learns from it, and never makes it again. A wise businessperson is one who finds a smart businessperson and learns from him how to avoid the mistakes he made.

Jim Abrams

#212 July 30

If it seems like you've got everything under control, you're just not going fast enough.

Mario Andretti

#213 July 31

In a world of change, either you make history or you are history.

Jack Daly

#214 August 1

Conduct quarterly, as a minimum, field training or coaching calls—riding shotgun—with each sales person.

#215 August 2

Things that get measured get done. Institute "success agreements" with each associate.

#216 August 3

One mistake will never kill you. The same mistake over and over will.

#217 August 4

It's not what you pay 'em; it's what they cost you.

#218 August 5

If the change inside your organization is slower than the change outside your company, the end is in sight.

Jack Welch

#219 August 6

Coach the top, and the bottom will spring up.

Bruce Woolpert

#220 August 7

Getting everyone to recruit provides new <u>and</u> renewed employees.

#221 August 8

Worry about the careers of those who work for you and then yours will thrive.

#222 August 9

When checking references, always ask, "Would you hire this person again?" Any answer other then "yes" is a "no."

#223 August 10

At the end of the day, you bet on people, not strategies.

Lawrence Bossidy

#224 August 11

If you want to be the first into a new territory, you cannot wait for a large amount of evidence.

Joel A. Barker

#225 August 12

If we want our salespeople to be firmly focused on the needs of the customer (and we do!), then our focus needs to be firmly on the needs of the salesperson.

Gerry Layo

#226 August 13

Those who do the work should have a say in how it's to be organized.

#227 August 14

Think of your P+L "expenses" as "investments," then calculate your expected ROI. This goes for staffing especially, given its size in relation to all other "expenses."

Jack Daly

#228 August 15

You cannot ask people to exercise broader judgement if their world is bounded by very narrow vision.

Robert Haas

#229 August 16

Your job is to make what you do obsolete, before your competition does it for you.

J. Howard Shelov

#230 August 17

Ninety-five percent of American managers today say the right thing. Five percent actually do it.

James O'Toole

#231 August 18

The best way to keep a good employee is to fire a bad one.

Bob Thompson

#232 August 19

We must look at only three things when measuring our people and they are based on a simple formula for success in all we do . . .
"Attitude + Skills + Activity = Success."

Gerry Layo

#233 August 20

It is important that people know what you stand for. It's equally as important that they know what you won't stand for.

Mary Waldrup

#234 August 21

If you're not training, you're not gaining.

#235 August 22

Think effectiveness with people; efficiency with things.

#236 August 23

Recruit for skills; hire for attitude.

#237 August 24

I don't know the key to success, but the key to failure is to try to please everyone.

Bill Cosby

#238 August 25

Learn the difference between running a meeting and leading a group.

#239 August 26

Running a company is very easy when you don't know how, but very difficult when you do.

Price Pritchett

#240 August 27

The bigger a man's head gets, the easier it is to fill his shoes.

Henry Courtney

#241 August 28

The best leaders are often the best listeners. They have an open mind. They are not interested in having their own way but finding the best way.

Wilfred Peterson

#242 August 29

You can do the work of two people, but you can't be two people. Instead, you have to inspire the next guy down the line to get him to inspire his people.

Lee Iacocca

#243 August 30

The most important thing you can do during an employment interview is plan your questions in advance. The second most important is to identify the answers you want to hear.

Bob Spence

#244 August 31

People without leaders are lost, but leaders without process are doomed!

Frank Pacetta

#245 September 1

The best motivation consists of getting a player to understand that his self-interest and the team's are inextricably bound up.

Walter Kiechel III

#246 September 2

I've rewarded failure by giving out awards to people when they've failed, because they took a swing. Keep taking swings . . . Punishing failure assures that no one dares.

Jack Welch

#247 September 3

Leaders are doers. Effective leaders first ask what needs to be done then they get their team to do it.

Peter Drucker

#248 September 4

To find the person you are looking for, define the person you are looking for.

#249 September 5

When preparing for the arrival of each new hire, consider the following: "If I were a new employee, what would be important for me to understand?"

#250 September 6

Require no report from a sales person for which leaders will not provide feedback to that individual.

#251 September 7

I have yet to find the man, however exalted his station, who did not do better work and put forth greater effort under a spirit of approval than a spirit of criticism.

Charles M. Schwab

#252 September 8

Within 30 minutes of arrival at a company, one can smell the company's culture—does yours smell of success or stink?

Jack Daly

#253 September 9

Compensation reviews and progress reviews should never be done at the same time.

#254 September 10

Build your business big enough to do the job, but "small" enough to care!

Cristi Cristich

#255 September 11

A progress review should be done whenever suggested—not by some arbitrary calendar schedule—but not less than quarterly in most cases.

#256 September 12

As leaders, we must find out what motivates each of our associates.

#257 September 13

Not praising good work and not facing up to problems are the most common errors in employee relations.

#258 September 14

I have often repented of speaking, but never of holding my tongue.

Xenocrates

#259 September 15

Salespeople measured on activity will produce activity. If you measure activities rather than outcomes, don't be surprised if you get lots of activity but no outcomes in terms of sales results. Measure results, not activities.

Neil Rackham

#260 September 16

Give a lot, expect a lot, and if you don't get it, prune.

Tom Peters

#261 September 17

Is there such a thing as overly recognized?

#262 September 18

A leader has two important characteristics; first, he is going somewhere; second, he is able to persuade other people to go with him.

Maximilien Francois Robespierre

#263 September 19

Have each sales support person spend minimally one day per quarter in the field on joint calls. Quid Pro Quo—have each sales person spend one day per quarter performing the functions in the sales support arena.

#264 September 20

A BHAG (Big Hairy Audacious Goal) engages people — it reaches out and grabs them in the gut. It is tangible, energizing, highly focused. People "get it" right away; it takes little or no explanation.

James C. Collins and Jerry I. Porras

#265 September 21

Establish a senior management customer call program.

#266 September 22

In real estate it's location, location, location. In business, it's differentiate, differentiate, differentiate.

Robert Goizueta

#267 September 23

It is not enough to ask which one of your departments might do a job better; ask whether anyone in the company should do the job at all.

Robert Kriegel

#268 September 24

Sports teams track and report performance for a reason. Sales leaders have the same reasons—Help your team to the top by letting them know where they stand.

Jack Daly

#269 September 25

Rewarding employees for their exceptional work is critical for keeping them motivated to continue to do their best.

Kenneth Blanchard

#270 September 26

For each new hire, deliver a positive experience on day one for the new associate to talk about with the "folks at home."

Jack Daly

#271 September 27

Are we, as leaders, here to be served or to serve?

#272 September 28

Create and support a sales advisory council that meets quarterly with senior management to jointly discuss selling initiatives.

#273 September 29

Always see people in their office, not yours. When somebody says: "Can I see you?" you say, "Sure, I'll be right over." There are two benefits: (1) you get out from behind your desk and walk the office halls, and (2) you can always leave when you want to. You are seen by others—always good for morale—and you usually learn one new thing every time around the office floor.

Dick Schlosberg

#274 September 30

Lifelong learning creates lifelong opportunities.

#275 October 1

Progress Review Preparation

- What do I want to communicate?
- Where do I want to focus suggested changes?
- How may I communicate this information so that the recipient will be receptive to it?
- What specific solution/goal may I offer and how may I assist the recipient to achieve his/her goal?

#276 October 2

Recognition programs are a very important element of your total compensation program.

Catherine Meek

#277 October 3

Motivation is what gets you started. Habit is what keeps you going.

Jim Ryan

#278 October 4

The relationship with a customer doesn't end with the purchase. It <u>begins</u> with the purchase. The purchase of an item should be the beginning of a long-term relationship that is fortified by verification of the quality of your service and delivery.

Thomas Winniger

#279 October 5

Once you recognize that the purpose of your life is not to serve your business, but that the primary purpose of your business is to serve your life, you can then go to work <u>on</u> your business, rather than <u>in</u> it.

#280 October 6

Share with everyone the "Big Picture" if you want their best performance.

#281 October 7

To build winners you must recognize what has to be done, and then try to do it. It's a matter of recognition, adjustment, and execution, in that order.

Vince Lombardi

#282 October 8

It's a fine thing to have ability, but the ability to discover ability in others is the true test.

David Armstrong

#283 October 9

The two resources your competitors can't copy are people and culture.

Eric Flamholtz

#284 October 10

The most significant mark of leadership is the willingness to make decisions and accept responsibility.

#285 October 11

The attitudes about time exhibited by the CEO of any organization will radiate throughout that organization.

#286 October 12

When wondering why it is that you have problems finding or keeping good salespeople, ask yourself one brutally honest question: "Would I work for me?"

Gerry Layo

#287 October 13

You can't delegate responsibility unless you can track performance.

#288 October 14

Any rewards, to be meaningful and motivating, have to be perceived as deserved, timely, and followed by prompt celebration.

#289 October 15

If top management sets the example, there is no need to broadcast the rules.

#290 October 16

Thank your people for their efforts and recognize them for performance. Recognition is ten times cheaper than compensation and 10 times more effective.

Kraig Kramers

#291 October 17

Leadership and learning are indispensable to each other.

John F. Kennedy

#292 October 18

Schedule an hour per week to think. Escape from the urgent and reclaim the important.

#293 October 19

Don't bother just to be better than your contemporaries or predecessors. Try to be better than yourself.

William Faulkner

#294 October 20

You don't delight the customer without delighting your employees. Can't happen.

Frank Pacetta

#295 October 21

You'll have trouble creating a new culture if you insist on doing it in ways that are consistent with the old one.

#296 October 22

Be careful with your actions. Your people will do one half of what you do right and twice what you do wrong.

Gerry Layo

#297 October 23

Marketing is about what people buy, not what you sell.

#298 October 24

Build a business that works not because of you, but without you. Simply put, your job is to prepare yourself and your business for growth.

#299 October 25

When performance is measured, performance improves.

#300 October 26

Do not follow where the path leads; rather, go where there is no path and leave a trail.

#301 October 27

Adversity has the effect of eliciting talents which in prosperous circumstances would have lain dormant.

Horace

#302 October 28

How can your company grow if your people don't?

Johan Beeckmans

#303 October 29

To keep good people in your organization, you have to get rid of the bad. You must show that you will not tolerate poor performance.

Bob Thomson

#304 October 30

People will listen to what you say, but their behavior will be changed by what you do.

#305 October 31

Culture change starts at the top, with the CEO. It is your behavior, more than any other factor, that sets the tone and thus affects the culture. Start out by looking at yourself. Think about your "bone-deep" beliefs.

Thomas Horton

#306 November 1

Nothing characterizes the successful organization so much as its willingness to abandon what has been long successful.

Theodore Levitt

#307 November 2

Success . . . My nomination for the single most important ingredient is energy well directed.

Louis B. Lundborg

#308 November 3

The one clear message is that "simplicity" in a company's product range, customer base, organization structure, and business system is key to corporate success.

Gunter Rommel

#309 November 4

Leadership is action, not position.

#310 November 5

It is only by understanding the business that you can delegate with any confidence. The trick, of course, is to delegate what you do understand, not what you don't.

Thomas Horton

#311 November 6

Bad service saves money and loses customers. Good service costs money and saves customers.

#312 November 7

My job is to get people to do what they don't want to do, so they can be what they've always wanted to be.

Tom Landry

#313 November 8

If there's a point to be made, either good or bad, do it dramatically. People will remember.

#314 November 9

To keep an organization young and fit don't hire anyone until everybody's so overworked they'll be glad to see the newcomer no matter where he sits.

Robert Townsend

#315 November 10

If you don't have an assistant, you are one.

Ralph Roberts

#316 November 11

Make no small plans for they have no magic to stir men's souls.

#317 November 12

Management's biggest problem is all the unemployed people on the payroll.

Anon

#318 November 13

The team with the best players almost always wins.

#319 November 14

The difference between a good company and a great company is the quality of the training.

Sharon Serpico Hanson

#320 November 15

Those not fired with enthusiasm will be fired with enthusiasm.

Vince Lombardi

#321 November 16

Hire slowly, fire quickly.

Ed Ryan

#322 November 17

The longest time in a manager's life is the time between the day you lose faith in someone, and the day you do something about it.

Jim Pratt

#323 November 18

Coach on the field, not in the locker room.

Jack Daly

#324 November 19

The occupational disease of a poor executive is an inability to listen.

Dr. Lydia Gibers

#325 November 20

What are your <u>systems</u> to ensure regular, ongoing, consistent recognition?

#326 November 21

Empowerment equates to action.

#327 November 22

Give up trying to grow the bottom line. Grow your people and your people will grow the bottom line.

Jim Sandstrom

#328 November 23

Either you run the day or the day runs you.

Jim Rohn

#329 November 24

In business, there's such a thing as an invaluable person, but no such thing as an indispensable one.

Malcolm Forbes

#330 November 25

When I started visiting the plants and meeting with employees, what was reassuring was the tremendous, positive energy in our conversations. One man said he'd been at Ford for twenty-five years and hated every minute of it—until he was asked for his opinion. He said that question transformed his job.

Donald Petersen

#331 November 26

Focused action beats intellectual brilliance every time in the marketplace of human affairs.

Mark Sanborn

#332 November 27

With so many ways to reward people, you may ask, "How do I decide how to reward each person?" The answer is simple: Ask them.

Michael Leboeu

#333 November 28

The best thing about setting a blistering pace is that it is easy to spot the stragglers.

Frank Pacetta

#334 November 29

If I had eight hours to chop down a tree, I'd spend six sharpening my axe.

Abraham Lincoln

#335 November 30

When creating an incentive, managers should focus on results, not activity.

George W. Walther

#336 December 1

The single most effective motivator of individuals in organizations is having clear, concrete performance objectives. If people know what is expected of them, they will attempt to do a good job.

John McNeil

#337 December 2

It is the CEO's responsibility to set business goals based on input from others. People rarely exceed goals they have set for themselves.

Clark Johnson

#338 December 3

Excitement is contagious. By allowing your emotions to be observed, you are giving permission to your people to let their feelings be shown, their fervor, their commitment. Once you capture the hearts of your people, their minds will follow . . . it's your job to energize your organization and to keep it energized.

Thomas Horton

#339 December 4

The bottom line is that leadership shows up in the inspired action of others. We traditionally have assessed leaders themselves. But maybe we should assess leadership by the degree to which people around leaders are inspired.

Dr. Jack Weber

#340 December 5

It's essential that whatever decisions you make, you make with conviction. You're not going to be a dynamic leader if you can't do that.

Ralph Lazarus

#341 December 6

The single greatest mistake a manager can make is to make a bad hire.

#342 December 7

A leader is one who knows the way, goes the way and shows the way.

John C. Maxwell

#343 December 8

If you're serious about wanting to recruit selling superstars, you'll have them written down, prioritized, and an ongoing campaign to "court them" toward your team.

Jack Daly

#344 December 9

Failure to recognize extra effort and success is a message that hard work is not all that important.

Frank Pacetta

#345 December 10

The macho image of leadership, associated with men like Vince Lombardi, Ross Perot, and Lee Iacocca, makes us forget that the real strength of a leader is the ability to elicit the strength of the group.

Richard Farson

#346 December 11

A company's business would increase 50% if you cleared the conference room of chairs.

W. F. Heneghan

#347 December 12

There is no difference between sports and business when it comes to the hiring process. Slipshod recruiting will give you a slipshod organization.

Frank Pacetta

#348 December 13

In every company, there are a handful of "gamebreaker" positions. Make sure you have superstars in each and every one.

Jerry Goldress

#349 December 14

During an interview, the candidate should talk 90% of the time. You are there to learn about the candidate and not vice versa.

Bob Spence

#350 December 15

You will never regret having spent too much time with your kids.

#351 December 16

I do not believe you can do today's job with yesterday's methods and be in business tomorrow.

Nelson Jackson

#352 December 17

What worked to motivate and to energize your team yesterday may not work today. The challenge is to constantly come up with something new.

Frank Pacetta

#353 December 18

Spend 80% of your development time with the best 20% of your people.

Bob Thompson

#354 December 19

If you want to change something, measure it. The measurement process leads to accountability, and without accountability, change will not occur.

Bob Beale

#355 December 20

To get results in business, make decisions democratically and implement dictatorially. Democratic implementation can be a disaster.

Peter Schutz

#356 December 21

Winning isn't everything, but wanting to win is.

Vince Lombardi

#357 December 22

People do what the boss inspects, not what he or she expects.

Maurice Mascarenhas

#358 December 23

There is no job that can't be delegated—except recognizing your people.

#359 December 24

The most important thing you can give your people is your time.

Larry King

#360 December 25

Nothing is ever gained by winning an argument and losing a customer.

C. F. Norton

#361 December 26

We should be as timely with our praise as we are with corrections.

#362 December 27

Spend at least 20% of your time talking with your customers. It's the only way you can know what the real world thinks about your company.

Jerry Goldress

#363 December 28

Six things an executive should never delegate:

Planning

Selecting the team

Monitoring their efforts

Motivating

Evaluating

Rewarding

#364 December 29

As we promote people up through the organization, we move them away from the customer. Too often our best talent is focused on the wrong mission. Get back to customer focus.

#365 December 30

As a true leader and a coach, your people should wake up in the morning and not "have" to come to work . . . they should get up and "get" to come to work!

Gerry Layo

#366 December 31

One day, an expert in time management was speaking to a group of business students and, to drive home a point, used an illustration those students will never forget. As he stood in front of the group of high powered overachievers he said, "Okay, time for a quiz." Then he pulled out a one-gallon, wide-mouthed mason jar and set it on the table in front of him. Then he produced about a dozen fist-sized rocks and carefully placed them, one at a time, into the jar. When the jar was filled to the top and no more rocks would fit inside, he asked, "Is this jar full?"

Everyone in the class said, "Yes."

Then he said, "Really?" He reached under the table and pulled out a bucket of gravel. Then he dumped some gravel in and shook the jar causing pieces of gravel to work themselves down into the space between the big rocks. Then he asked the group once more, "Is the jar full?"

By this time the class was on to him. "Probably not," one of them answered.

"Good!" he replied. He reached under the table and brought out a bucket of sand. He started dumping the sand in the jar and it went into all of the spaces left between the rocks and the gravel. Once more he asked the question, "Is this jar full?"

"No!" the class shouted.

Once again he said, "Good." Then he grabbed a pitcher of water and began to pour it in until the jar was filled to the brim. Then he looked at the class and asked, "What is the point of this illustration?"

One eager beaver raised his hand and said, "The point is, no matter how full your schedule is, if you really try hard you can always fit some more things in it!"

"No," the speaker replied, "that's not the point. The truth this illustration teaches us is: If you don't put the big rocks in first, you'll never get them in at all."

What are the 'big rocks' in your life?

Your children; Your loved ones; Your education; Your dreams; A worthy cause; Teaching or mentoring others; Doing things that you love; Time for yourself; Your health; Your significant other.

Remember to put these BIG ROCKS in first or you'll never get them in at all. If you sweat the little stuff you'll fill your life with little things you worry about that don't really matter and you'll never have the real quality time you need to spend on the big, important stuff. So, tonight, or in the morning, when you are reflecting on this short story, ask yourself this question: What are the 'big rocks' in my life? Then, put those in your jar first.

ABOUT THE AUTHOR
JACK DALY

Jack Daly brings 20 plus years of field proven experience—from a starting base with the CPA firm of Arthur Andersen to the CEO level of several national companies. Jack has participated at the senior executive level in four de novo businesses, two of which were subsequently sold to the Wall Street firms of Solomon Brothers and First Boston.

As the head of sales and production, Jack has led sales forces numbering in the thousands, operating out of hundreds of offices nationwide. His leadership experience was shaped at the Fleet Mortgage Group, Security Pacific Bank, Glenfed Mortgage Corporation, Home Mortgage Access Corporation and Evans Products Corporation.

A few highlights include:

➢ Headed sales for America's 4th largest national mortgage banker, as well as the $15 billion California division of the nation's 5th largest savings bank.

➢ In 1985 relocated from the East Coast to California to lead a mortgage company start-up. As CEO, Jack spurred growth to

22 branches operating in 40 states, with 750 employees, generating $350 million per month in mortgages. Over the initial 3 year period, reported earnings of $42 million.

Jack was born and raised in Philadelphia, Pennsylvania, and currently resides in San Juan Capistrano, California. Jack's education includes an MBA from Wilmington College, a BS from LaSalle University, and the rank of Captain in the U.S. Army.

Jack currently wears two hats: COO (Chief Opportunity Officer) of Platinum Capital Group, and CEO (Chief Energizing Officer) of Professional Sales Coach, Inc. His previous books include Daly Sales Motivators.

PLATINUM CAPITAL GROUP

Platinum Capital Group operates as a full-service national mortgage company, headquartered in Southern California. The eight-year-old privately held company garnered significant recognition in 1998 as a fast growth/high performance industry leader, to include: Ernst & Young Entrepreneur of the Year; Top Ten on the Inc. 500; Blue Chip Enterprise Award from the U.S. Chamber of Commerce; and ranked #1 Fastest Growing Privately Held Company in Los Angeles.

17101 Armstrong Avenue
Suite 200, Irvine, CA 92614
(949) 221-0800
www.PlatinumCapital.com

PROFESSIONAL SALES COACH, INC.

Professional Sales Coach, Inc. (PSC), is a sales and sales leadership training and consulting firm. PSC's core business is coaching companies to greater sales and profits. As a result of demand worldwide, Jack Daly delivers keynote presentations for industry conferences and company sales and customer events.

Jack's custom-designed programs deliver results. On several occasions Jack has spoken to YEO Universities and Inc. Magazine conferences, garnering highest rated speaker honors.

Professional Sales Coach's cutting difference is "speaking from experience."

5842 La Jolla Corona Drive
La Jolla, CA 92037
(888) 298-6868
jackdpsc@aol.com

Professional Sales Coach Training Tools by Jack Daly

		With Workbook *(Please circle your selection in these columns)*	Without Workbook	Quantity
Building A World-Class Sales Organization (Sales Management - Live - 3 hours)	A) Video	$150	N/A	
	B) Audio Cassette	$40	$30	
	C) CD	$50	$40	
Coaching Companies To Greater Sales & Profits (Sales Management Enhanced - Live - 2 hours)	A) Audio Cassette	$40	$30	
	B) CD	$50	$40	
Smart Selling Through Value (Sales Training - Live - 3 hours)	D) Video	$150	N/A	
	E) Audio Cassette	$40	$30	
	F) CD	$50	$40	
Relationship Selling (Sales Training - Studio Recorded - 6 hours)	G) Audio Cassette	$75	N/A	
Achieving Leadership Excellence (Sales Management - Studio Recorded - 6 hours)	H) Audio Cassette	$75	N/A	
Books etc	Coaching Companies to Greater Sales & Profits (Book)	N/A	$15	
	Daly Sales Motivators (Book)	N/A	$15	
	Daly Sales Motivators (Perpetual Calendar)	N/A	$15	
	Building A World-Class Sales Organization	N/A	$15	
	Smart Selling	N/A	$15	
	Marketing Magic	N/A	$15	
Package Specials	** Videos "A" + "D"	$250	N/A	
	** Audios "B" + "E"	$70	$50	
	** CD's "C" + "F"	$80	$60	

** Less 10% Discount on orders over $250.00 **   **SUB-TOTAL:** _____

Applicable California sales tax, shipping & handling will be added to invoice.   **TOTAL PURCHASE AMOUNT:** _____

PLEASE FILL OUT THE PAYMENT OPTIONS AND SHIPPING INFORMATION ON THE BACK SIDE OF THIS FORM

PLEASE FILL OUT THE PRODUCT ORDER FORM ON THE OTHER SIDE OF THIS PAGE

**For product information or
speaking inquiries, please
contact:**

Jack Daly

Professional Sales Coach, Inc.
5842 La Jolla Corona Drive
La Jolla, California 92037

Telephone: (888) 298-6868
Fax: (858) 454-5481
www.ProfessionalSalesCoach.net

TOTAL AMOUNT
OF PURCHASE

$

☐ **Yes!** *Please add my name to your distribution list for a free Email Sales Management Newsletter.*

Name _____ Date _____

Company _____

Street Address _____

City _____ State _____ Zip _____

Day Phone _____ Email _____

☐ VISA
☐ MC   Card No. / / / / / / / / / / / / / / / /
☐ AMEX

Exp. date _____ / _____ Signature _____